# THE MEETING MAKER

*A Journey Journal For Recovery*

Copyright © 2024 by Write 2 Recovery
All rights reserved

Chapin Keith Publishing
Daleville, VA. 24083
www.Chapinkeith.com

Publisher's Cataloging-in-Publication Data

Names: Write 2 Recovery
Title: The Meeting Maker

Identifiers: ISBN 979-8-9893575-9-8

Journal concept and quotes by Beth Poulin

Cover and book design by Asya Blue Design

*For Catherine-My-Catherine, whose guidance to put pen to paper is always a suggestion of love, not a mandate of process. And for those who don't yet have that person in their lives, let these blank pages be a launching point to become whole, healed and recovered.*

To Fellows, Friends & Freedom Seekers -

Many a Sponsor have said "we listen to learn, and we share to heal", and of those many, ALL have meant it. This Journal will allow you to do both at your own pace and practice - congratulations on an investment in your Recovery.

The blank space ahead is a canvas for you to document a new life of peace in bloom, and a new legacy of Service in motion.

These pages offer an opportunity to focus on tasks at hand, moments that matter, and each Meeting in progress. The sections are designed to organize your thoughts as you spotlight your priorities and de-escalate your fears. Allow it not to be a burden, but a best friend in defining your spectrum of Recovery.

We live in a world where distractions have the potential to derail our destiny – any resource we can use to support ourselves should be seen as a manifestation of self-worth, not as a sign of weakness.

Welcome this tool as a fluid opportunity to structure your Sobriety and your Spirit. Each volume filled will provide both insight and hindsight in allowing you to look back, track AND attack mysteries and miracles along the way.

It will also gift you the chance to recognize the accomplishments of your Fellows, remain open to having your own related unique thoughts on Program-related literature and absorb the invaluable intuitions of those that have come before you.

Because thoughts that better your own life today might help save someone else's tomorrow.

Because the heavier these pages get with your words, the lighter your Soul will feel.

**BECAUSE WE ALL HAVE THE WRITE TO RECOVER.**

DATE _____ TIME _____
LOCATION _____

**MEETING TYPE & CHAIRPERSON**

_____
_____
_____
_____
_____
_____

**PRE-MEETING VIBE**

_____
_____
_____
_____
_____
_____

NEWCOMERS/
VISITORS

TOPIC

**WHAT AM I MOVED TO SHARE?**

_____
_____
_____
_____
_____
_____
_____

**FROM MY FELLOWS:**

**ANNOUNCEMENTS**

**MILESTONES**

**POST-MEETING VIBE**

**DON'T FORGET TO...**

**NOTES**

DATE _____  TIME _____

LOCATION _____

## MEETING TYPE & CHAIRPERSON

_____
_____
_____
_____
_____
_____

## PRE-MEETING VIBE

_____
_____
_____
_____
_____
_____

### NEWCOMERS/ VISITORS

### TOPIC

## WHAT AM I MOVED TO SHARE?

_____
_____
_____
_____
_____
_____

**FROM MY FELLOWS:**

**ANNOUNCEMENTS**

**MILESTONES**

**POST-MEETING VIBE**

**DON'T FORGET TO...**

**NOTES**

DATE _____  TIME _____

LOCATION _____

## MEETING TYPE & CHAIRPERSON

_____
_____
_____
_____
_____

### NEWCOMERS/VISITORS

### PRE-MEETING VIBE

_____
_____
_____
_____
_____

### TOPIC

## WHAT AM I MOVED TO SHARE?

_____
_____
_____
_____
_____
_____

**FROM MY FELLOWS:**

**ANNOUNCEMENTS**

**MILESTONES**

**POST-MEETING VIBE**

**DON'T FORGET TO...**

**NOTES**

DATE                                              TIME

LOCATION

## MEETING TYPE & CHAIRPERSON

NEWCOMERS/
VISITORS

## PRE-MEETING VIBE

TOPIC

## WHAT AM I MOVED TO SHARE?

**FROM MY FELLOWS:**

**ANNOUNCEMENTS**

**MILESTONES**

**POST-MEETING VIBE**

**DON'T FORGET TO...**

**NOTES**

DATE _____  TIME _____

LOCATION _____

## MEETING TYPE & CHAIRPERSON

_____
_____
_____
_____
_____

### NEWCOMERS/VISITORS

## PRE-MEETING VIBE

_____
_____
_____
_____
_____

### TOPIC

## WHAT AM I MOVED TO SHARE?

_____
_____
_____
_____
_____
_____

**FROM MY FELLOWS:**

**ANNOUNCEMENTS**

**MILESTONES**

**POST-MEETING VIBE**

**DON'T FORGET TO...**

**NOTES**

"Sobriety Allows For Tolerance, Recovery Allows For Empathy."

## NOTES AND ADDITIONAL VIBES

DATE _____  TIME _____

LOCATION _____

## MEETING TYPE & CHAIRPERSON

## NEWCOMERS/VISITORS

## PRE-MEETING VIBE

## TOPIC

## WHAT AM I MOVED TO SHARE?

**FROM MY FELLOWS:**

**ANNOUNCEMENTS**

**MILESTONES**

**POST-MEETING VIBE**

**DON'T FORGET TO...**

**NOTES**

DATE _____  TIME _____
LOCATION _____

## MEETING TYPE & CHAIRPERSON

_____
_____
_____
_____
_____
_____

### NEWCOMERS/ VISITORS

## PRE-MEETING VIBE

_____
_____
_____
_____
_____
_____

### TOPIC

## WHAT AM I MOVED TO SHARE?

_____
_____
_____
_____
_____
_____

**FROM MY FELLOWS:**

**ANNOUNCEMENTS**

**MILESTONES**

**POST-MEETING VIBE**

**DON'T FORGET TO...**

**NOTES**

DATE                                              TIME

LOCATION

## MEETING TYPE & CHAIRPERSON

### NEWCOMERS/ VISITORS

### PRE-MEETING VIBE

### TOPIC

## WHAT AM I MOVED TO SHARE?

**FROM MY FELLOWS:**

**ANNOUNCEMENTS**

**MILESTONES**

**POST-MEETING VIBE**

**DON'T FORGET TO...**

**NOTES**

DATE _____ TIME _____

LOCATION _____

## MEETING TYPE & CHAIRPERSON

_____

_____

_____

_____

_____

_____

**NEWCOMERS/ VISITORS**

## PRE-MEETING VIBE

_____

_____

_____

_____

_____

_____

**TOPIC**

## WHAT AM I MOVED TO SHARE?

_____

_____

_____

_____

_____

_____

**FROM MY FELLOWS:**

**ANNOUNCEMENTS**

**MILESTONES**

**POST-MEETING VIBE**

**DON'T FORGET TO...**

**NOTES**

DATE _____  TIME _____

LOCATION _____

## MEETING TYPE & CHAIRPERSON

## NEWCOMERS/ VISITORS

## PRE-MEETING VIBE

## TOPIC

## WHAT AM I MOVED TO SHARE?

**FROM MY FELLOWS:**

**ANNOUNCEMENTS**

**MILESTONES**

**POST-MEETING VIBE**

**DON'T FORGET TO...**

**NOTES**

"Unless You Collect A Paycheck From The Local Sanitation Board, Do NOT Haul Around Past Garbage All Day."

## NOTES AND ADDITIONAL VIBES

DATE _____  TIME _____

LOCATION _____

## MEETING TYPE & CHAIRPERSON

_____
_____
_____
_____
_____

### NEWCOMERS/ VISITORS

## PRE-MEETING VIBE

_____
_____
_____
_____
_____

### TOPIC

## WHAT AM I MOVED TO SHARE?

_____
_____
_____
_____
_____
_____

**FROM MY FELLOWS:**

**ANNOUNCEMENTS**

**MILESTONES**

**POST-MEETING VIBE**

**DON'T FORGET TO...**

**NOTES**

DATE _____  TIME _____

LOCATION _____

## MEETING TYPE & CHAIRPERSON

_____
_____
_____
_____
_____

### NEWCOMERS/ VISITORS

### TOPIC

## PRE-MEETING VIBE

_____
_____
_____
_____
_____

## WHAT AM I MOVED TO SHARE?

_____
_____
_____
_____
_____
_____

**FROM MY FELLOWS:**

**ANNOUNCEMENTS**

**MILESTONES**

**POST-MEETING VIBE**

**DON'T FORGET TO...**

**NOTES**

DATE _____ TIME _____

LOCATION _____

## MEETING TYPE & CHAIRPERSON

### NEWCOMERS/ VISITORS

### TOPIC

## PRE-MEETING VIBE

## WHAT AM I MOVED TO SHARE?

**FROM MY FELLOWS:**

**ANNOUNCEMENTS**

**MILESTONES**

**POST-MEETING VIBE**

**DON'T FORGET TO...**

**NOTES**

DATE     TIME

LOCATION

## MEETING TYPE & CHAIRPERSON

### NEWCOMERS/ VISITORS

### TOPIC

## PRE-MEETING VIBE

## WHAT AM I MOVED TO SHARE?

**FROM MY FELLOWS:**

**ANNOUNCEMENTS**

**MILESTONES**

**POST-MEETING VIBE**

**DON'T FORGET TO...**

**NOTES**

DATE _____  TIME _____

LOCATION _____

## MEETING TYPE & CHAIRPERSON

_____
_____
_____
_____
_____
_____

### NEWCOMERS/VISITORS

_____

## PRE-MEETING VIBE

_____
_____
_____
_____
_____
_____

### TOPIC

_____

## WHAT AM I MOVED TO SHARE?

_____
_____
_____
_____
_____
_____
_____

**FROM MY FELLOWS:**

**ANNOUNCEMENTS**

**MILESTONES**

**POST-MEETING VIBE**

**DON'T FORGET TO...**

**NOTES**

"Allow Yourself To Move Away From Knee-Jerk Reactions, And Towards Knee-Slap Moments."

## NOTES AND ADDITIONAL VIBES

DATE _____   TIME _____

LOCATION _____

## MEETING TYPE & CHAIRPERSON

_____
_____
_____
_____
_____

## PRE-MEETING VIBE

_____
_____
_____
_____
_____

NEWCOMERS/ VISITORS

TOPIC

## WHAT AM I MOVED TO SHARE?

_____
_____
_____
_____
_____
_____

**FROM MY FELLOWS:**

**ANNOUNCEMENTS**

**MILESTONES**

**POST-MEETING VIBE**

**DON'T FORGET TO...**

**NOTES**

DATE _____ TIME _____

LOCATION _____

## MEETING TYPE & CHAIRPERSON

_____
_____
_____
_____
_____
_____

### NEWCOMERS/VISITORS

## PRE-MEETING VIBE

_____
_____
_____
_____
_____
_____

### TOPIC

## WHAT AM I MOVED TO SHARE?

_____
_____
_____
_____
_____
_____
_____

**FROM MY FELLOWS:**

**ANNOUNCEMENTS**

**MILESTONES**

**POST-MEETING VIBE**

**DON'T FORGET TO...**

**NOTES**

DATE _____  TIME _____

LOCATION _____

## MEETING TYPE & CHAIRPERSON

_____
_____
_____
_____
_____
_____

NEWCOMERS/
VISITORS

## PRE-MEETING VIBE

_____
_____
_____
_____
_____
_____

TOPIC

## WHAT AM I MOVED TO SHARE?

_____
_____
_____
_____
_____
_____

**FROM MY FELLOWS:**

**ANNOUNCEMENTS**

**MILESTONES**

**POST-MEETING VIBE**

**DON'T FORGET TO...**

**NOTES**

DATE _____   TIME _____

LOCATION _____

## MEETING TYPE & CHAIRPERSON

_____
_____
_____
_____
_____

### NEWCOMERS/ VISITORS

## PRE-MEETING VIBE

_____
_____
_____
_____
_____

### TOPIC

## WHAT AM I MOVED TO SHARE?

_____
_____
_____
_____
_____
_____

**FROM MY FELLOWS:**

**ANNOUNCEMENTS**

**MILESTONES**

**POST-MEETING VIBE**

**DON'T FORGET TO...**

**NOTES**

DATE                                            TIME

LOCATION

## MEETING TYPE & CHAIRPERSON

### NEWCOMERS/ VISITORS

## PRE-MEETING VIBE

### TOPIC

## WHAT AM I MOVED TO SHARE?

**FROM MY FELLOWS:**

**ANNOUNCEMENTS**

**MILESTONES**

**POST-MEETING VIBE**

**DON'T FORGET TO...**

**NOTES**

"**Sometimes Recovery Calls For Tough Love, Because This Is Tough Sh*t.**"

## NOTES AND ADDITIONAL VIBES

DATE                                              TIME

LOCATION

## MEETING TYPE & CHAIRPERSON

### NEWCOMERS/ VISITORS

### PRE-MEETING VIBE

### TOPIC

## WHAT AM I MOVED TO SHARE?

**FROM MY FELLOWS:**

**ANNOUNCEMENTS**

**MILESTONES**

**POST-MEETING VIBE**

**DON'T FORGET TO...**

**NOTES**

DATE _____  TIME _____

LOCATION _____

## MEETING TYPE & CHAIRPERSON

_____
_____
_____
_____
_____

## PRE-MEETING VIBE

_____
_____
_____
_____
_____

### NEWCOMERS/ VISITORS

### TOPIC

## WHAT AM I MOVED TO SHARE?

_____
_____
_____
_____
_____
_____

**FROM MY FELLOWS:**

**ANNOUNCEMENTS**

**MILESTONES**

**POST-MEETING VIBE**

**DON'T FORGET TO...**

**NOTES**

DATE _____ TIME _____

LOCATION _____

## MEETING TYPE & CHAIRPERSON

_____
_____
_____
_____
_____

## PRE-MEETING VIBE

_____
_____
_____
_____
_____

### NEWCOMERS/VISITORS

### TOPIC

## WHAT AM I MOVED TO SHARE?

_____
_____
_____
_____
_____
_____

**FROM MY FELLOWS:**

**ANNOUNCEMENTS**

**MILESTONES**

**POST-MEETING VIBE**

**DON'T FORGET TO...**

**NOTES**

DATE  TIME

LOCATION

## MEETING TYPE & CHAIRPERSON

### NEWCOMERS/ VISITORS

## PRE-MEETING VIBE

### TOPIC

## WHAT AM I MOVED TO SHARE?

**FROM MY FELLOWS:**

**ANNOUNCEMENTS**

**POST-MEETING VIBE**

**DON'T FORGET TO...**

**NOTES**

**MILESTONES**

DATE _____  TIME _____

LOCATION _____

## MEETING TYPE & CHAIRPERSON

_____
_____
_____
_____
_____

### NEWCOMERS/VISITORS

## PRE-MEETING VIBE

_____
_____
_____
_____
_____

### TOPIC

## WHAT AM I MOVED TO SHARE?

_____
_____
_____
_____
_____
_____

**FROM MY FELLOWS:**

**ANNOUNCEMENTS**

**MILESTONES**

**POST-MEETING VIBE**

**DON'T FORGET TO...**

**NOTES**

> "Sit With Uncomfortable, Stand For Recovery, Walk Through Regret."

## NOTES AND ADDITIONAL VIBES

DATE _____  TIME _____

LOCATION _____

## MEETING TYPE & CHAIRPERSON

_____
_____
_____
_____
_____
_____

### NEWCOMERS/ VISITORS

## PRE-MEETING VIBE

_____
_____
_____
_____
_____
_____
_____

### TOPIC

## WHAT AM I MOVED TO SHARE?

_____
_____
_____
_____
_____
_____

**FROM MY FELLOWS:**

**ANNOUNCEMENTS**

**MILESTONES**

**POST-MEETING VIBE**

**DON'T FORGET TO...**

**NOTES**

DATE						TIME

LOCATION

## MEETING TYPE & CHAIRPERSON

NEWCOMERS/
VISITORS

## PRE-MEETING VIBE

TOPIC

## WHAT AM I MOVED TO SHARE?

**FROM MY FELLOWS:**

**ANNOUNCEMENTS**

**MILESTONES**

**POST-MEETING VIBE**

**DON'T FORGET TO...**

**NOTES**

DATE _____  TIME _____

LOCATION _____

## MEETING TYPE & CHAIRPERSON

_____
_____
_____
_____
_____
_____

## NEWCOMERS/VISITORS

_____
_____
_____
_____
_____

## PRE-MEETING VIBE

_____
_____
_____
_____
_____
_____

## TOPIC

_____
_____
_____
_____

## WHAT AM I MOVED TO SHARE?

_____
_____
_____
_____
_____
_____
_____

**FROM MY FELLOWS:**

**ANNOUNCEMENTS**

**MILESTONES**

**POST-MEETING VIBE**

**DON'T FORGET TO...**

**NOTES**

DATE _____  TIME _____
LOCATION _____

## MEETING TYPE & CHAIRPERSON

_____
_____
_____
_____
_____

## PRE-MEETING VIBE

_____
_____
_____
_____
_____

### NEWCOMERS/ VISITORS

### TOPIC

## WHAT AM I MOVED TO SHARE?

_____
_____
_____
_____
_____
_____

**FROM MY FELLOWS:**

**ANNOUNCEMENTS**

**MILESTONES**

**POST-MEETING VIBE**

**DON'T FORGET TO...**

**NOTES**

DATE _____ TIME _____

LOCATION _____

## MEETING TYPE & CHAIRPERSON

_____
_____
_____
_____
_____
_____

### NEWCOMERS/VISITORS

_____
_____
_____

## PRE-MEETING VIBE

_____
_____
_____
_____
_____
_____

### TOPIC

_____
_____
_____

## WHAT AM I MOVED TO SHARE?

_____
_____
_____
_____
_____
_____
_____

**FROM MY FELLOWS:**

**ANNOUNCEMENTS**

**MILESTONES**

**POST-MEETING VIBE**

**DON'T FORGET TO...**

**NOTES**

> "When You Struggle With Believing In Your Higher Power, Just Focus On Their Belief In YOU."

## NOTES AND ADDITIONAL VIBES

DATE                                    TIME

LOCATION

## MEETING TYPE & CHAIRPERSON

### NEWCOMERS/ VISITORS

### PRE-MEETING VIBE

### TOPIC

## WHAT AM I MOVED TO SHARE?

## FROM MY FELLOWS:

## ANNOUNCEMENTS

## POST-MEETING VIBE

## DON'T FORGET TO…

## NOTES

## MILESTONES

DATE                                          TIME

LOCATION

## MEETING TYPE & CHAIRPERSON

NEWCOMERS/
VISITORS

## PRE-MEETING VIBE

TOPIC

## WHAT AM I MOVED TO SHARE?

**FROM MY FELLOWS:**

**ANNOUNCEMENTS**

**MILESTONES**

**POST-MEETING VIBE**

**DON'T FORGET TO...**

**NOTES**

DATE  TIME

LOCATION

## MEETING TYPE & CHAIRPERSON

## PRE-MEETING VIBE

NEWCOMERS/
VISITORS

TOPIC

## WHAT AM I MOVED TO SHARE?

**FROM MY FELLOWS:**

**ANNOUNCEMENTS**

**MILESTONES**

**POST-MEETING VIBE**

**DON'T FORGET TO...**

**NOTES**

DATE _____ TIME _____

LOCATION _____

## MEETING TYPE & CHAIRPERSON

_____
_____
_____
_____
_____
_____

**NEWCOMERS/ VISITORS**

## PRE-MEETING VIBE

_____
_____
_____
_____
_____
_____

**TOPIC**

## WHAT AM I MOVED TO SHARE?

_____
_____
_____
_____
_____
_____
_____

**FROM MY FELLOWS:**

**ANNOUNCEMENTS**

**MILESTONES**

**POST-MEETING VIBE**

**DON'T FORGET TO...**

**NOTES**

DATE                                              TIME

LOCATION

## MEETING TYPE & CHAIRPERSON

### NEWCOMERS/ VISITORS

### TOPIC

## PRE-MEETING VIBE

## WHAT AM I MOVED TO SHARE?

**FROM MY FELLOWS:**

**ANNOUNCEMENTS**

**MILESTONES**

**POST-MEETING VIBE**

**DON'T FORGET TO...**

**NOTES**

"Our Favorite Advice To Give Others Is That Which We Are Afraid To Follow Ourselves. Feel That."

## NOTES AND ADDITIONAL VIBES

DATE _____   TIME _____

LOCATION _____

## MEETING TYPE & CHAIRPERSON

_____
_____
_____
_____
_____
_____

### NEWCOMERS/ VISITORS

## PRE-MEETING VIBE

_____
_____
_____
_____
_____

### TOPIC

## WHAT AM I MOVED TO SHARE?

_____
_____
_____
_____
_____
_____
_____

**FROM MY FELLOWS:**

**ANNOUNCEMENTS**

**MILESTONES**

**POST-MEETING VIBE**

**DON'T FORGET TO...**

**NOTES**

DATE _____ TIME _____

LOCATION _____

## MEETING TYPE & CHAIRPERSON

_____
_____
_____
_____
_____
_____

### NEWCOMERS/ VISITORS

## PRE-MEETING VIBE

_____
_____
_____
_____
_____

### TOPIC

## WHAT AM I MOVED TO SHARE?

_____
_____
_____
_____
_____
_____
_____

**FROM MY FELLOWS:**

**ANNOUNCEMENTS**

**MILESTONES**

**POST-MEETING VIBE**

**DON'T FORGET TO...**

**NOTES**

DATE _____ TIME _____

LOCATION _____

## MEETING TYPE & CHAIRPERSON

_____

_____

_____

_____

_____

### NEWCOMERS/ VISITORS

## PRE-MEETING VIBE

_____

_____

_____

_____

_____

_____

### TOPIC

## WHAT AM I MOVED TO SHARE?

_____

_____

_____

_____

_____

_____

**FROM MY FELLOWS:**

**ANNOUNCEMENTS**

**MILESTONES**

**POST-MEETING VIBE**

**DON'T FORGET TO...**

**NOTES**

DATE

TIME

LOCATION

## MEETING TYPE & CHAIRPERSON

## PRE-MEETING VIBE

### NEWCOMERS/ VISITORS

### TOPIC

## WHAT AM I MOVED TO SHARE?

**FROM MY FELLOWS:**

**ANNOUNCEMENTS**

**MILESTONES**

**POST-MEETING VIBE**

**DON'T FORGET TO...**

**NOTES**

DATE                                          TIME

LOCATION

## MEETING TYPE & CHAIRPERSON

NEWCOMERS/
VISITORS

## PRE-MEETING VIBE

TOPIC

## WHAT AM I MOVED TO SHARE?

**FROM MY FELLOWS:**

**ANNOUNCEMENTS**

**MILESTONES**

**POST-MEETING VIBE**

**DON'T FORGET TO...**

**NOTES**

> "Anger Is Like Any Other Drug – It Will Get You A High, But Will Leave You Exhausted."

## NOTES AND ADDITIONAL VIBES

DATE  TIME

LOCATION

## MEETING TYPE & CHAIRPERSON

NEWCOMERS/ VISITORS

## PRE-MEETING VIBE

TOPIC

## WHAT AM I MOVED TO SHARE?

**FROM MY FELLOWS:**

**ANNOUNCEMENTS**

**MILESTONES**

**POST-MEETING VIBE**

**DON'T FORGET TO...**

**NOTES**

DATE _____ TIME _____

LOCATION _____

## MEETING TYPE & CHAIRPERSON

_____
_____
_____
_____
_____
_____

## NEWCOMERS/VISITORS

## PRE-MEETING VIBE

_____
_____
_____
_____
_____
_____

## TOPIC

## WHAT AM I MOVED TO SHARE?

_____
_____
_____
_____
_____
_____

**FROM MY FELLOWS:**

**ANNOUNCEMENTS**

**MILESTONES**

**POST-MEETING VIBE**

**DON'T FORGET TO...**

**NOTES**

DATE _____ TIME _____

LOCATION _____

## MEETING TYPE & CHAIRPERSON

_____
_____
_____
_____
_____
_____

**NEWCOMERS/ VISITORS**

## PRE-MEETING VIBE

_____
_____
_____
_____
_____

**TOPIC**

## WHAT AM I MOVED TO SHARE?

_____
_____
_____
_____
_____
_____
_____

**FROM MY FELLOWS:**

**ANNOUNCEMENTS**

**MILESTONES**

**POST-MEETING VIBE**

**DON'T FORGET TO...**

**NOTES**

DATE _____ TIME _____

LOCATION _____

## MEETING TYPE & CHAIRPERSON

## NEWCOMERS/VISITORS

## TOPIC

## PRE-MEETING VIBE

## WHAT AM I MOVED TO SHARE?

**FROM MY FELLOWS:**

**ANNOUNCEMENTS**

**MILESTONES**

**POST-MEETING VIBE**

**DON'T FORGET TO...**

**NOTES**

DATE     TIME

LOCATION

## MEETING TYPE & CHAIRPERSON

## NEWCOMERS/ VISITORS

## PRE-MEETING VIBE

## TOPIC

## WHAT AM I MOVED TO SHARE?

**FROM MY FELLOWS:**

**ANNOUNCEMENTS**

**MILESTONES**

**POST-MEETING VIBE**

**DON'T FORGET TO...**

**NOTES**

"You'll Realize You're Almost Around The Track When You Have Some Bumps And Bruises From Hurdles."

## NOTES AND ADDITIONAL VIBES

DATE _____  TIME _____

LOCATION _____

## MEETING TYPE & CHAIRPERSON

_____
_____
_____
_____
_____
_____

### NEWCOMERS/VISITORS

## PRE-MEETING VIBE

_____
_____
_____
_____
_____

### TOPIC

## WHAT AM I MOVED TO SHARE?

_____
_____
_____
_____
_____
_____
_____

**FROM MY FELLOWS:**

**ANNOUNCEMENTS**

**MILESTONES**

**POST-MEETING VIBE**

**DON'T FORGET TO...**

**NOTES**

DATE _____ TIME _____

LOCATION _____

## MEETING TYPE & CHAIRPERSON

_____
_____
_____
_____
_____
_____

## PRE-MEETING VIBE

_____
_____
_____
_____
_____
_____
_____

### NEWCOMERS/ VISITORS

### TOPIC

## WHAT AM I MOVED TO SHARE?

_____
_____
_____
_____
_____
_____
_____

**FROM MY FELLOWS:**

**ANNOUNCEMENTS**

**MILESTONES**

**POST-MEETING VIBE**

**DON'T FORGET TO...**

**NOTES**

DATE                                               TIME

LOCATION

## MEETING TYPE & CHAIRPERSON

### NEWCOMERS/ VISITORS

### PRE-MEETING VIBE

### TOPIC

## WHAT AM I MOVED TO SHARE?

**FROM MY FELLOWS:**

**ANNOUNCEMENTS**

**MILESTONES**

**POST-MEETING VIBE**

**DON'T FORGET TO...**

**NOTES**

DATE                                          TIME

LOCATION

## MEETING TYPE & CHAIRPERSON

### NEWCOMERS/ VISITORS

### TOPIC

## PRE-MEETING VIBE

## WHAT AM I MOVED TO SHARE?

**FROM MY FELLOWS:**

**ANNOUNCEMENTS**

**MILESTONES**

**POST-MEETING VIBE**

**DON'T FORGET TO...**

**NOTES**

DATE _____   TIME _____

LOCATION _____

## MEETING TYPE & CHAIRPERSON

_____
_____
_____
_____
_____
_____

### NEWCOMERS/VISITORS

## PRE-MEETING VIBE

_____
_____
_____
_____
_____
_____

### TOPIC

## WHAT AM I MOVED TO SHARE?

_____
_____
_____
_____
_____
_____
_____

**FROM MY FELLOWS:**

**ANNOUNCEMENTS**

**MILESTONES**

**POST-MEETING VIBE**

**DON'T FORGET TO...**

**NOTES**

"We Are Not On Trial For Our Pasts, We Are On Deck For Our Futures."

## NOTES AND ADDITIONAL VIBES